How To Convince Your Parents You Can...

Care For A Pet Hamster

Carol Parenzan Smalley

Mitchell Lane
PUBLISHERS
P.O. Box 196
Hockessin, Delaware 19707
Visit us on the web: www.mitchelllane.com
Comments? email us: mitchelllane@mitchelllane.com

Mitchell Lane
PUBLISHERS

Printing   1   2   3   4   5   6   7   8   9

A Robbie Reader/How to Convince Your Parents You Can...

Care for a Kitten
Care for a Pet Bunny
Care for a Pet Chameleon
Care for a Pet Chimpanzee
Care for a Pet Chinchilla
Care for a Pet Ferret
Care for a Pet Guinea Pig
Care for a Pet Hamster
Care for a Pet Hedgehog
Care for a Pet Horse

Care for a Pet Mouse
Care for a Pet Parrot
Care for a Pet Racing Pigeon
Care for a Pet Snake
Care for a Pet Sugar Glider
Care for a Pet Tarantula
Care for a Pet Wolfdog
Care for a Potbellied Pig
Care for a Puppy
Care for a Wild Chincoteague Pony

Library of Congress Cataloging-in-Publication Data
Smalley, Carol Parenzan, 1960–
    Care for a pet hamster / by Carol Parenzan Smalley.
        p. cm. — (A Robbie reader. How to convince your parents you can...)
    Includes bibliographical references and index.
    ISBN 978-1-58415-804-2 (library bound)
    1. Hamsters as pets—Juvenile literature. I. Title. II. Title: How to convince your parents you can—care for a pet hamster.
    SF459.H3S62 2010
    636.935'6—dc22
                                                                                                2009027351

ABOUT THE AUTHOR: Carol Parenzan Smalley thought she wanted a tent for her ninth birthday, until she passed a pet store in the mall. A petite Siamese kitten mewed at her and her dad through the display window. Now, they had to convince Carol's mom that a kitten would be a perfect birthday present. That was 1969, and the Siamese kitten did come home with Carol. She named her Dutchess, and this precious feline loved her and her family for 17 years. Later, two more Siamese kittens came to live with Carol—for 17 and 21 years! Carol knows that owning any pet—whether it's a hamster or a Siamese kitten—takes a lot of time and hard work every day for many years. But if you have the time and patience, a pet can be a wonderful addition to a family.

Today, Carol shares her life in upstate New York with yet two more Siamese kittens. Their names are Junie B. and Amber Brown, for two of her daughter's favorite storybook characters. You can see photos of "the double-trouble girls" at www.CarolSmalley.com.

PUBLISHER'S NOTE: The facts on which this story is based have been thoroughly researched. Documentation of such research is on page 29. While every possible effort has been made to ensure accuracy, the publisher will not assume liability for damages caused by inaccuracies in the data, and makes no warranty on the accuracy of the information contained herein.

Special thanks to Tammy S. Hagadorn, LVT, A.S., Veterinary Technology, B.S., Biology, and M.S., Education, and Office Manager, Fort Plain Animal Hospital, Fort Plain, New York.

TABLE OF CONTENTS

Chapter One 5
What's Peeking from Your Pocket?

Chapter Two 9
The Desert Dweller

Chapter Three 15
Selecting a Healthy Hamster

Chapter Four 21
Caring for Your Critter

Chapter Five 25
A Hamster at Home or at School

Find Out More 29
    Books 29
    Works Consulted 29
    On the Internet 30
Glossary 31
Index 32

Words in **bold** type can be found in the glossary.

Although hamsters don't require a lot of care, they do need to be cared for well. If you do not handle them gently, or if you frighten them, they may pee on you, bite or nip you, or even run away as a warning that they are not happy.

The American Academy of Pediatrics recommends that children be at least five years old before owning a hamster. Hamsters have been known to carry Salmonella. Young children can catch this disease more easily than older kids, and they often put their hands in their mouths. You should always wash your hands after handling any pet.

Chapter One

WHAT'S PEEKING FROM YOUR POCKET?

Would you like a quiet pet that can sleep in your shirt pocket? Would you like to train a small animal? Do you think it would be fun to feed a furry critter from your fingers? If so, a hamster might be the perfect pet for you.

But before you gather your allowance or birthday money to buy a hamster or try to convince your parents that a hamster is the perfect pet, there's much you need to know.

The hamster is a **nocturnal** (nok-TUR-nul) animal that sleeps during the day. It plays, eats, and explores while most animals (including humans) are sleeping at night. It is a petite (puh-TEET) **mammal** that requires a small cage, a quiet place, and limited care. Caring for a hamster can help you learn pet-care responsibilities on a small scale. Your parents won't have to pester you to take care of your pet.

Hamsters are sometimes called "pocket pets." They like to hide or hang out in pockets. They may hoard, or hide, food in a pocket to eat later!

When you're in school, your hamster will be home resting. While you're away, no one needs to take your hamster for a walk or exercise it in your backyard. When your homework is done in the evening, your hamster will be ready to play with you.

At home, you may be able to share hamster-care responsibilities with your siblings. But if you're an only child, you can care for the hamster yourself. It's really not that hard and does not take a lot of time.

fun **FACTS**

Hamsters are rodents. They belong to the same animal family—Rodentia (roh-DEN-shee-uh)—as mice, rats, guinea pigs, squirrels, porcupines, gophers, and beavers. Unlike your front teeth, a rodent's front teeth—called incisors (in-SY-zerz)—never stop growing. Rodents must chew constantly to keep their incisors trimmed.

Do you live in an apartment that doesn't allow cats and dogs? It may allow hamsters and other small pets.

You should ask yourself: Are there different kinds of hamsters? How long do they live? What do they eat? Can you find hamsters in the wild? What size cage do they need? Do they play with toys? If my hamster gets sick, what will I do? Are they expensive to care for? Do hamsters like to play with other hamsters?

Where can you learn the answers to these questions and much more? Right here! Turn to chapter 2 and meet the subfamily of **rodents** known as Cricetinae (kry-SEE-tih-nay), more commonly called hamsters.

Not only do Siberian hamsters like to kiss, they also like to escape from wire cages and under closed doors. These hamsters, also called Dwarf Winter White Russian hamsters, grow to about three inches in length.

 **Chapter Two**

THE DESERT DWELLER

In the wild, hamsters live in the desert, where it is hot during the day and cool at night. They live in **steppes**, which are dry grassland areas.

They rest during the day in underground homes—called burrows—where it's cooler and they are protected from **predators**. At night, they **forage** (FOR-ij) for food. They may hoard, or save, it for later.

Hamster coat colors and markings are similar to those in their native **habitat**. They are **camouflaged** (KAM-uh-flahjd) with their natural surroundings.

If the weather turns too cold, hamsters can go into a deep sleep called torpor. When temperatures fall below 46°F, hamsters may sleep soundly, only to wake every five to six days to eat and drink.

The wild hamster's natural sleeping and eating cycle is the same for **domestic** hamsters. A pet hamster may become sluggish and less active if the room it is in becomes cooler than normal.

Throughout Europe, Central Asia, Russia, Mongolia, and China, there are 18 **species** of hamsters living in the wild. There are no wild hamsters in North America.

*fun***FACTS**

In the wild, a hamster can run up to five miles each night in search of food. Although domestic hamsters don't have to run to search for food, they do need to exercise.

Some of the more common species are the Syrian (SEER-ee-un) hamster, the Chinese hamster, and the Roborovski (ruh-buh-ROF-skee) hamster. The most common pet hamster is the Syrian, or golden, hamster.

Hamsters' bodies are round and solid. They can squeeze through tight spaces. Because their whiskers are as long as their bodies are wide, they act like a ruler. A hamster will know if it can fit through a space if its whiskers can slide through the opening. Hamsters have poor eyesight. Their whiskers help them to "see" by feeling their way, especially in dark places.

Hamsters are different lengths. The Syrian hamster is about seven inches long. A dwarf hamster is shorter (1 to 3 inches long), and a European hamster is longer (about 12 inches long).

Their size may also determine their lifespan. Most hamsters live about two to three years. A European hamster can live up to eight years.

In the wild, hamsters rely on their senses for survival. They smell to find food. They also mark their territories using scent glands on the sides of their bodies. Other hamsters smell the markings and know to stay away.

Not all hamsters like other hamsters. In general, female hamsters are much more aggressive than male hamsters.

Roborovski dwarf hamsters have "white eyebrows." These tiny—but quick—pets grow to the size of a human adult's thumb. They are one of the few hamsters that will eat meat and insects in addition to vegetables and fruits.

Some hamsters are **sociable** (SOH-shuh-bul). For example, Dwarf Campbell's Russian hamsters like to live in pairs or small groups. Other hamsters, such as the Roborovski and Chinese hamsters, like to live in colonies. But don't put two Syrian or European hamsters together. They will fight each other to defend their territories. They are **solitary** (SAH-lih-tayr-ee) animals.

Even solitary hamsters need to reproduce. For a short time, the male (buck) and the female (doe) come together to make babies (pups). Only 16 days later, a litter of 6 to 10 hamsters is born.

The mother **lactates** (LAK-tayts), or makes and provides milk, for her litter for up to five weeks. She may have up to 16 nipples on her underside to feed her young family. Babies will start to eat solid food in about one week. Male hamsters do not help to rear the young.

Three snuggling Roborovski hamsters. Roborovski hamster litters are small, but some hamster mothers can deliver up to 24 babies in a single litter!

Two Chinese dwarf hamsters prepare to run on a wheel. Chinese dwarf hamsters have long tails. Other species have very short tails.

Hamsters can reproduce at the age of eight weeks. After having a litter of pups, a female hamster can become pregnant again just one week later. She can have babies until she is 18 months old.

Because hamsters reproduce easily, in many parts of the world, hamsters are not considered pets but pests. They can overrun villages, nest inside homes and buildings, and chew electrical wiring. But in other areas, hamsters may be **endangered** (en-DAYN-jerd) and need protection.

A hamster's hair can be shades of white, gray, or black. It can have golden hues, such as honey, yellow, blond, or cream. Sometimes a hamster's coat displays reddish colors, such as rust, cinnamon, or even copper. Hamster fur may be shiny or satiny. Its coat may be long (called a teddy bear coat) or wavy (a Rex coat). Hamsters can even be hairless! A healthy hamster's coat is never knotted.

SELECTING A HEALTHY HAMSTER

Although hamsters live in the wild, you never want to take a hamster from its natural environment or purchase one that has been captured. This is not fair to the wild hamster, and in some places, it is illegal to keep wild animals as pets.

One place you may find hamsters that need a good home is an animal shelter. Sometimes, people must move and can't take their pets with them. Perhaps their pets had more babies than their humans could care for properly. People place their pets, including hamsters, in shelters, hoping that someone else will adopt and love their animals.

You may want to visit a pet store to look for a pet hamster. Pet stores purchase hamsters from **breeders**. Breeders match male and female hamsters to create hamsters with specific coat colors, patterns, and textures.

The tortoiseshell pattern is black, gray, gold, and cinnamon mixed with yellow splotches. The banded pattern has a white band around the hamster's middle, while his belly is white. A white-bellied hamster has a white belly but no white band. Hamsters that are white with colored spots on their heads and backs are dominant-spot hamsters.

The best time to look at hamsters is in the evening when they are awakening from their daytime slumber. Hamsters should not be sold until they are weaned, usually at five weeks of age. Healthy hamsters have bright eyes and are alert. They have healthy teeth that are not too long or too short.

Their front paws should have four healthy toes and claws. Their front paws act like hands to hold their food. Their back paws should have five toes and claws. Their back paws are used for grooming. They use all their paws to cling and climb. Their claws should not be too long or too short.

If possible, you should handle the hamster and play with it. It may be shy or frightened of you, but this will change as you get to know each other better.

Before you bring your hamster home, you will need special equipment. You will need a home for your hamster. One common hamster home has a wire-cage top and a deep, plastic basin. Carefully measure the space between the wire bars. The maximum distance between the bars will depend on your

hamster's size. Hamsters can squeeze through spaces that are too large.

Some hamsters live in aquarium tanks. The aquarium should not be smaller than 10 gallons. You will need a screen top to fit securely on top of the aquarium. You may want to place a weight on top so that your hamster cannot escape.

Creative hamster owners make **hamsterariums** for their pets. A hamsterarium is like a hamster's natural home. It has a dirt mixture for burrowing, and multiple rooms, such as a bathroom, eating area, and exercise room, connected by tunnels.

Your hamster will also need private sleeping quarters (perhaps a small box). Your hamster home requires bedding, such as wood shavings, crushed

Some hamster owners create fancy hamster homes. This boy's hamster can explore plastic tunnels, much like he would explore underground tunnels in the wild.

corncobs, or chopped hay or straw. Never use pine or cedar in a hamster's home. These can make it ill.

Your hamster needs daily exercise. You can purchase an exercise wheel, with a solid wheel for safety, for inside its home. If your hamster has long hair, you may need to trim it so that it doesn't get caught in the wheel.

You may also want to get an exercise ball that it can roll around on the floor. If you get a ball, be careful of steps and stairs. Some hamsters may become stressed inside the ball. Keep a close eye on your hamster.

You may also want to get other toys for your hamster. These could include balls, ladders, tunnels, and chew circles. Depending on the size of your hamster, it may not fit through tunnels! Ask someone at the pet store to help you choose these items for your pet.

Once each week, clean your hamster's cage. First, put your hamster in a safe place. Wearing gloves, remove the dirty bedding. Then wash the cage with warm water and mild soap, and add clean bedding. Wash the dishes and toys, too.

Hamsters drink a lot of water. Purchase a water dropper bottle for inside your hamster's home. They also need a heavy dish for food. You should buy food made just for hamsters. You should also add fresh fruits, vegetables, and nuts.

Before you take your hamster home, visit your **veterinarian** (vet-ruh-NAYR-ee-un) for a healthy pet check and pet-care advice. If you will have more than one hamster or if your hamster will have playmates, you should also discuss **spaying** or **neutering** your pets to prevent unwanted pups.

Syrian hamsters can store grain—up to half of their body weight—in their cheeks. The average male hamster weighs about four ounces. That would be two ounces of grain!

Chapter Four 4

CARING FOR YOUR CRITTER

In the wild, hamsters forage for plant food, such as grains, grasses, roots, berries, and fruit. They also eat insects. This means they are **omnivores** (OM-nih-voors). They forage for food that is **nutritious** (noo-TRIH-shus), and carry it back to their homes in their cheek pouches.

At home, you are the hamster's **nutritionist!** You control its diet. In addition to the hamster food you purchased at the pet store, you can also give your hamster fruits (such as apples and pears), vegetables (such as broccoli, carrots, celery, peas, and leafy lettuce), seeds (such as pumpkin and sunflower), nuts (such as crushed almonds), grains (such as rolled oats), grasses (such as alfalfa and clover), and even meats (such as small amounts of turkey or chicken).

Never give your pet hamster onions, potatoes, raw beans, garlic, or rhubarb. These are poisonous to hamsters.

You may want to scatter some of the food in its cage so that it can forage as it would in nature. Your hamster may also hide its food. Fresh food may spoil and smell. You'll want to check its home daily for food that is starting to decay.

Always provide fresh, clean water for your hamster in its water dropper bottle. Replace the water every day.

Do not place your hamster's home in direct sunlight, near a heat source, or in a draft. Your hamster needs a quiet place, away from noisy televisions and computer games. Talk quietly to your hamster. Do not scream or use a high-pitched voice.

Be careful if you have other pets. Cats and dogs may harm your hamster if they are allowed to come together, even in friendly play.

Hamsters don't need baths, but if they have long hair, they may need to be brushed. You can use a soft, clean toothbrush to groom your hamster.

Your hamster will probably use one corner of its home as its bathroom. Scoop the dirty bedding daily to prevent smells. Change all of the bedding weekly, or as needed. You should handle your hamster gently, lifting it with two hands. Don't squeeze!

Your hamster may become ill and need veterinary care. If your hamster coughs, sneezes, or has a runny nose, it may have a cold. If you see fleas,

Feeding your hamster a wide variety of colorful fruits and vegetables will keep it healthy.

mites, or ticks, it may need to be treated for **parasites** (PAYR-uh-syts).

Some hamsters develop "wet tail," which can include diarrhea (dy-uh-REE-uh) and a loss of appetite. This is serious and needs immediate attention by your veterinarian. Your hamster's cheek pouches can also become infected by sharp or sticky food.

If your hamster is limping, it may have injured itself in a fall. Your veterinarian can tell you if a bone is broken or if other treatment is necessary.

And, if your hamster just isn't acting like itself—if it lies around, has limited interest in food, starts to lose its hair, or has overgrown teeth—see your veterinarian.

Hamsters that like the company of other hamsters enjoy sharing tight spaces, just like they do in the wild. Be sure to check your shoes before inserting any toes!

Chapter Five

A HAMSTER AT HOME OR AT SCHOOL

Owning a pet hamster is a big responsibility. Do you think you can do it? Do your parents think you can be a responsible pet owner? If you live in an apartment, will your landlord allow you to have it?

Before you and your parents make a decision about owning a pet hamster, you should learn as much as you can about the care of hamsters. You can sit and read this book together. You can also visit your local library to find additional books about hamsters and other pets. In the back of this book is a list of reading resources and web sites you may find helpful.

Your veterinarian's office is another good resource. The people who work there can give you suggestions or guidance about owning a pet hamster. They can help you prepare a pet budget. With a pet budget, you can figure out how much your hamster and its equipment will cost. You can also include the cost of regular veterinary care and checkups. Your vet

can tell you what it might cost if you have a pet emergency. Who will pay for your pet's expenses? What can you do to help pay for the cost of your pet?

You can also learn about hamsters from other hamster owners and animal fans. Check with your local 4-H office to see if there is a club that focuses on small animal care. You may be able to take a 4-H pet-care course or see other hamsters at a hamster show before you make a decision about which hamster to buy or adopt. You may meet breeders at these shows who can also answer questions.

Depending on your age, you may be able to volunteer at your local animal shelter and help care for hamsters that are up for adoption. This is good practice for owning a pet.

If you can't have a hamster at home, you may be able to convince your teacher to have a classroom

fun FACTS

Hamsters first arrived in U.S. pet stores in 1938. In 2008, hamsters were the fifth most popular household pet, with more than one million hamsters living in U.S. homes. (The top four were cats, dogs, birds, and rabbits.) By 2008, there were 41 percent more hamsters in homes than there were in 2001.

fun FACTS

A hamster's sense of smell is so strong, it may mistake food scents on your hands as food! Be sure to wash your hands thoroughly before you handle your hamster. You wouldn't want your hamster to think your fingers were french fries!

pet. Hamsters can be good reading buddies. They never give away the story's ending. Taking care of hamsters lets you practice your math skills, too. For example, what percentage of raw food, like fruits and vegetables, do you feed them each day? How much does it cost each month to keep a hamster?

You and your classmates can share in the hamster's care. Whose turn is it to feed the pet? Who will clean its cage? Who gets to hold and play with the hamster? Who will take the hamster home each weekend and during school breaks?

You can talk to your classmates about hamsters and hamster care. This book can be one of your sources. You could create a hamster chore chart so that everyone understands the care that is required. You could also share the book *My Pet Hamster & Gerbils* by LeeAnne Engfer with them. It is about a

As you and your pocket pet become more comfortable with each other, your hamster may choose to snooze in your arms. When he or she does fall asleep, it's a sign of trust. You have become the perfect pet owner!

hamster named Lightning II that lives in a fourth-grade classroom.

Whether you own a hamster yourself or it becomes a classroom project, owning a pet is a big responsibility. The more you learn about your pet, the better caregiver you will be. You and your desert dweller may enjoy years of fun with each other.

FIND OUT MORE

Books

Barnes, Julia. *101 Facts About Hamsters.* Lydney, England: Ringpress Books, Ltd., 2002.

Page, Gill. *I Am Your Hamster.* Columbus, Ohio: Waterbird Books, 2004.

Stevens, Kathryn. *Hamsters (Pet Care for Kids).* Mankato, Minnesota: Child's World, 2009.

Waters, Jo. *The Wild Side of Pet Hamsters.* Chicago: Raintree, 2005.

Works Consulted

This book is based on the author's interview with Tammy S. Hagadorn, LVT, A.S., Veterinary Technology, B.S., Biology, and M.S., Education, and Office Manager, Fort Plain Animal Hospital, Fort Plain, New York, September 8, 2008, and on the following sources:

Associated Press. "Kids Want a Hamster? Ask Your Doctor First: Pediatricians Warn about Health Risks from Unusual Pets." *MSNBC,* October 7, 2008. http://www.msnbc.msn.com/id/27035470/

Carpenter, James W., DVM; Ted Y. Mashima, DVM; and David J. Rupiper, DVM. *Exotic Animal Formulary.* Manhattan, Kansas: Graystone Publishing, 1996.

Carroll. David L. *The ASPCA Complete Guide to Pet Care.* New York: PLUME (Penguin Group), 2001.

Dale, Steve. "Pet Census." *USA Weekend,* January 27, 2008. http://www.usaweekend.com/08_issues/080127/080127pets-census.html.

FIND OUT MORE

Hamsters. 4-H Publication No. 277.

Hillyer, Elizabeth V., DVM; and Kathryn E. Quesenberry, DVM. *Ferrets, Rabbits, and Rodents: Clinical Medicine and Surgery.* Philadelphia: W.B. Saunders Co. (Harcourt), 1997.

Siino, Betsy Sikora. *The Hamster: An Owner's Guide to a Happy Healthy Pet.* New York: Howell Book House (A Simon & Schuster Macmillan Company), 1997.

Von Frisch, Otto. *Hamsters: Everything about Purchase, Care, Nutrition, Breeding, Behavior, and Training.* Hauppauge, N.Y.: Barron's Educational Series, Inc., 1997.

On the Internet

Hamster Heaven
   http://www.hamster-heaven.com/

Hamsterific!
   http://www.hamsterific.com/

Hamsters as Pets
   http://exoticpets.about.com/cs/hamsters/a/
   hamstercare.htm

Humane Society of the United States:
   How to Care for Hamsters
   http://www.hsus.org/pets/pet_care/rabbit_horse_and_
   other_pet_care/how_to_care_for_hamsters.html

GLOSSARY

breeder—A person who keeps animals and sells the babies.

camouflage (KAM-uh-flahj)—Having skin, fur, or clothing that blends with the natural surroundings.

domestic (doh-MES-tik)—Living in a person's home; not wild.

endangered (en-DAYN-jerd)—At risk of becoming extinct.

forage (FOR-ij)—To search the ground for food.

habitat (HAB-ih-tat)—Where an animal or plant lives.

hamsterarium (ham-ster-AYR-ee-um)—An enclosure for domestic hamsters that is similar to their home in nature.

incisors (in-SY-zurs)—The sharp teeth in the front of the mouth used for chewing or cutting.

lactate (LAK-tayt)—To produce and provide milk for babies.

mammal—Warm-blooded animal that produces milk for its young.

neuter—To make a male animal unable to reproduce.

nocturnal (nok-TUR-nul)—To be awake and active at night.

nutritionist (noo-TRIH-shuh-nist)—A person who studies and recommends food to eat.

nutritious (noo-TRIH-shus)—Rich in vitamins and minerals.

omnivore (OM-nih-voor)—An animal that eats both plants and animals.

parasite (PAYR-uh-syt)—A tiny animal that depends on another animal to live.

predator (PREH-duh-tur)—An animal that hunts other animals for food.

rodents (ROH-dents)—Mammals that have long, continuously growing incisors.

sociable (SOH-shuh-bul)—Liking the company of others.

solitary (SAH-lih-tayr-ee)—Preferring to live alone.

spay—To make a female animal unable to reproduce.

species (SPEE-sheez)—A group of animals that are similar and that can have babies together.

steppe (STEP)—An area that is grassy, dry, and cold.

veterinarian (vet-ruh-NAYR-ee-un)—An animal doctor.

INDEX

4-H   26
animal shelter   15, 26
apartment living   7, 25
bedding   17, 22, 26, 27
body   20
breeder   15, 26
burrow   9, 17
camouflage   9
care   4, 5, 6, 7, 15, 19, 23, 25–27
cheek pouches   20, 21, 23
children's literature,
    hamsters in   27
classroom pet   26–28
claws   16,
coat   9, 14, 15, 16, 18, 22, 23
Cricetinae   7
desert   9, 28
diet
    food   9, 10, 11, 12, 16, 19, 20,
        21, 22, 23, 26, 27
    water   19, 22
equipment   16, 25
    aquarium   17
    cage   5, 7, 12, 16, 19, 22, 27
    hamsterarium   17
exercise   6, 10, 13, 17, 18
eyes   10, 16
forage   9, 21, 22
hamster, Chinese   10, 12, 13
hamster, domestic   9, 10
hamster, Dwarf Campbell
    Russian   12
hamster, Dwarf Winter White
    Russian   8, 10
hamster, European   11
hamster, Roborovski   10, 11, 12
hamster, Siberian   8

hamster, Syrian (golden)   10, 12,
    20
hamsters, wild   7–9, 10, 11, 15, 21
handling   4, 27
hoarding   6, 9, 20
home   9, 17, 18, 19, 21, 22
illness   7, 18, 23
incisor   7
lactation   12
mammal   5, 12
natural territory   9, 28
nocturnal   5
parasites   23
paws   16
popularity   26
predator   9
purchasing   5, 15, 26
reproduction
    gestation   12
    litter size   12
    neuter   19
    spay   19
resources   19, 23, 25, 26, 27
Rodentia   7
rodents   7
senses   10, 11, 22, 27
size   8, 10–11, 12, 18
sleep   5, 9, 17, 22, 28
social skills   12
solitary   12
species   10–11, 12
steppes   9
tails   13
teeth   7, 16, 23
torpor   9
toys   18
veterinarian   19, 23, 25–26
whiskers   10